The Shark and the Sunken Ship

Written by Alison Hawes

Illustrated by Jan Smith

Big Skeleton and Little Skeleton were out swimming when they spotted a sunken ship.

"I want to have a look in the ship,"
said Little Skeleton.

The ship was bursting with riches!
There were lots of jars of coins.

"What a lot of coins and riches," said
Big Skeleton. "I cannot pick them all up!"

Little Skeleton spotted a harp.
Big Skeleton said, "Come and help
me lift the coins. You might snap the
strings on the harp!"

So Little Skeleton and Big Skeleton
lifted the coins up on deck.

But a shark spotted the coins!
"I will have some of that for my
supper," he said.

The skeletons went back up on deck.
"We are going to be rich!" they said.

But the skeletons were in for a shock!
The coins were not there!

Then they had a fright when a shark
swam up to the sunken ship.

"I had the coins for my supper, but I feel so sick, I wish I had not. I am going to have fish for supper from now on!"